But are they learning?

But are they learning?

A commonsense parents' guide to assessment and grading in schools

Richard Stiggins and Tanis Knight

Assessment Training Institute
50 SW 2nd Ave., Suite 300
Portland, OR 97204

Project Coordinator: Nancy Bridgeford
Editor: Robert Marcum
Production: Jennifer Dickey
Design & Typesetting: Diana Stout Yates
Cover Design: Cheryl Nangeroni
Photo Credits: Image Club Graphics

Printed in the USA
ISBN 0-9655101-1-5
Library of Congress Catalog Card Number 97-71224

Additional copies of this book may be ordered from the Assessment Training Institute. Discounts are available for bulk orders. Call 503-228-3060 or 800-480-3060.

Table of contents

Acknowledgments

We would like to thank the following parents for reviewing early drafts of this guide and for helping us speak clearly on behalf of quality assessment and the well-being of students: Michele Anciaux, Cheryl Duke, Dean Hummel, Jim Jamieson, Cyndie Schmeiser, Tia Wulff, and Rose Mary Knapp. In addition to sharing their reactions as parents, some of these reviewers also brought an educator's experience to the evaluation and revision process: Michele is Parent Involvement Director of the Washington State PTA; Jim is Principal of Willamette High School, Eugene, Oregon; Cyndie is Vice President of the American College Testing Program, Iowa City, Iowa; Tia is an elementary teacher in Portland, Oregon, and Rose Mary is a high school library and media specialist in Camas, Washington. It is only with their help that we were able to view the classroom assessment process from a full range of important perspectives.

Welcome!

This guide arises from our experiences both as parents and professional educators. As parents, we have witnessed the effects of sound and unsound classroom assessment practices in the motivation and academic success of our own children. While some of their teachers have had clear expectations, assessed their students accurately, and have used assessments to motivate students to strive for excellence, others, unfortunately, have not.

As professional educators and educational researchers, we have studied the classroom assessment process in great depth for many years. We have documented teachers who are supremely proficient at teaching and assessing the achievement of students, and others who have great difficulty assessing accurately. We find that many assessment problems in the classroom arise because teachers and administrators are not aware of sound practices, the result of a general lack of assessment training in their professional preparation.

Please understand from the outset that our goal is not to point out potential shortcomings in classroom assessment practices in order to indict schools or educators. Rather, we seek to use our professional expertise to alert you as fellow parents: Do not simply assume that all is well with assessment and evaluation in your child's school or district. Your local assessment house may be in order, or it may not be. Our goals are to provide you with background on the potential assessment dangers, suggest questions you can ask in your schools, and advise you on how to interpret and act on the answers you receive.

We know that, as a group, teachers are dedicated professionals striving to provide their students (our children) with the most productive learning experiences. However, the evolution of school practices and of teacher and administrator training in the United States over the past fifty years has left the vast majority of educators without the tools or expertise needed to do their assessment, evaluation, and grading jobs. Further, most teachers readily admit this, and seek opportunities to fill this gap in their professional preparation to practice. In fact, the mission of the Assessment Training Institute is to assist them in this endeavor.

You can help, too, but not by assessing the achievement of your children or by helping teachers assess accurately. Teachers themselves must do that job. You can help by supporting the allocation of needed resources to help your local educators do a good job of assessing. We seek partnerships — ways for parents to work within local schools and communities to encourage and support teachers as they pursue what professional development they need to help them align assessments with the needs of their students.

We know parents' aspirations for their children vary greatly among families and that schools are public institutions responsible for meeting all of those diverse needs. But we also believe in a common thread that holds us all together: Each student must *want* to succeed academically in order to find success in school.

Any student who gives up on school, on their teachers, or on themselves as learners represents an unacceptable loss. Teachers who rely on quality assessments and who use them wisely to diagnose student needs, keep track of growth, and motivate students to succeed are in the best position to prevent such losses.

Teachers proficient in the design and effective use of quality assessments understand that the primary motivation to succeed must come from within the student. They know how to use assessments to light that inner flame. School and family must fan that flame together by expecting students to become proficient in monitoring their own achievement and by helping students to understand what to do when they are not "getting it." Our philosophy is, any students who leave school unable to tell if they have done well are not yet an academic success, because they cannot apply rigorous standards to evaluating the quality of their own work.

We seek to promote a much higher proportion of academic winners in the future of our schools than we have seen in the past. This requires educators committed to making sure students are learning. It also requires learners who know through self-assessment when they are or are not succeeding — and who study in environments in which admitting the need for help is not ridiculed or seen as a sign of weakness. And finally, it requires *your* help, in the form of collaboration between home and school in which you help your children take personal responsibility for overcoming those academic weaknesses. This guide describes your role in that partnership.

Rick Stiggins and Tanis Knight
April 1997

Why inquire about classroom assessment?

If you're reading this book, you're probably already a parent who cares a great deal about education in general, and about your children's education in particular. The chances are you interact with the teachers and administrators in your school, trying to stay informed about the curriculum, day-to-day instruction, and overall school quality. However, even as a committed parent, you may be wondering, "How does classroom assessment make a difference in my child's learning? Mostly, I'm concerned about issues that have a direct bearing on my child's academic performance. Is this assessment topic really that important?" As a partial answer to that question, consider the real-life stories of these three parents:

> *My fourth-grade daughter, Lily, an excellent student, came home from school very upset on report card day. On the verge of tears, she showed me a card containing all B grades. I was startled, because there had been no prior indication from the teacher that Lily's performance had changed. Lily did not understand why she had received all B's, saying that she had received no grade lower than an A for the marking period. I decided to meet with her teacher and find out the other side of the story.*

I found that the "other side of the story" was pretty simple and straight-forward. The teacher felt that Lily was capable of doing more and better work than she was doing. I asked the teacher whether Lily had earned any grade lower than an A for the marking period. The teacher said, "No." I asked if she had explained to Lily that she would not be grading on actual performance, but on the basis of her judgment of Lily's potential. Flustered, the teacher repeated that she did not want Lily to take her studies for granted. By giving her all B's, she felt Lily would push herself to keep improving. My response was straightfor-ward. "How," I asked, "could a kid like Lily value the grading process if she didn't understand the basis for her grade or how you deter-mined it?" I received no satisfactory answer.

I was not surprised when Lily received all A's for the next marking period and continued to do so for the rest of the year. Neither Lily nor I will ever know if she really earned these grades. I'm as upset that Lily might be getting unearned A's as I was that she had received unfair B's. I feel as if I have little valid feedback about how well Lily is actually learning and performing. ■

Mike, our high schooler, is learning French, and is excited about his growing proficiency. His teacher seems very competent. She empha-sizes the development of speaking proficiency, and relies heavily on assessments in which she listens to students speak and subjectively evaluates their skills. Mike is struggling to master spoken French.

His teacher also uses paper and pencil tests to be sure her students are mastering the foundations of vocabulary and grammatical struc-ture. Mike does very well on these — he always has, in almost all subjects. But because his performance skills are lagging, his grades suffer. In fact, he's become so centered on getting good grades that we fear he will become discouraged and give up French to maintain his grade point average. We don't want that! However, we just don't know what to say to the teacher, or to Mike. What should we do? ∎

Our daughter Suzanne, a tenth grader, received a midterm report saying she was getting a D+ in biology. She earned an A on the first unit test and did well on other assignments, and was at a loss to explain the grade. I requested a meeting with the teacher to discuss the progress report.

"[She] . . . was at a loss to explain the grade."

Without checking his records, the teacher said that Suzanne must not be learning the material or her grade would be higher. He was sorry, he said, that he didn't have time to work with her individually — because he faces 180 students each day.

The teacher entered her name into his computer gradebook and the screen listed entries leading to an average of 69 percent. He pointed out that his cutoff scores transform this percentage into a D+, so Suzanne's progress report is correct. However, as I scanned the screen I noticed the details:

First unit test	95%
Unit lab report	85%
Second unit test	85%
Unit lab report	0%
Midterm Average:	69%

I asked about the "zero percent." The teacher said that if a test or report is missing the computer enters a zero into the computation of the grade average. "But," I pointed out, "Suzanne understands the material and is performing well on the required assessments." The teacher seemed genuinely surprised at the reason for the low grade, agreeing that the rest of the record was very good. "Then how," I asked, "did you conclude earlier that she is not learning the *material?" The teacher retreated to his claim of having too little time to know every student.*

We discussed the difference between learning the material and completing the assignments, confronting the confusion that can result when a simple summary grade like "D+" blends the two in ways that parents aren't given the opportunity to understand. If Suzanne isn't learning the material, we would respond in one way. If she's not completing the work, our response would be completely different. We want to help, but the reporting process needs to let us know how!

As parents and guardians, we are responsible for the academic well-being of our children during their school years. But in these cases, what do these concerned parents do? They're frustrated, and have lost confidence in their child or their child's teacher. They sense that teachers have difficulty developing credible grading systems that everyone clearly understands. They also now wonder about the meaning and impact of grades. As for the teachers, they too become distressed and, naturally, a bit defensive. Their well-intentioned attempts to use grades to motivate students have not had the results they expected. But what do they do next?

Do these examples sound familiar? Can you relate them to situations you or your child have experienced? Like you, the people in the vignettes need to understand the differences between sound and unsound classroom assessment and grading practices. They need to know what to do next to avoid poisoning the parent-teacher or student-teacher relationship. The importance of knowing at least the basics of good assessment in today's complex and changing educational environment cannot be overstated.

In its simplest terms, *classroom assessment* refers to the procedures teachers use to track students' ongoing achievement — to evaluate academic progress day to day as instruction unfolds. This definition has broad implications when we think about school effectiveness, for it is only through effective assessment that teachers reveal to us that they truly understand what they want their students to learn. In a way, assessment completes the contract between families and their schools. It is the only way for schools to validate to students, teachers, and parents just what students have learned and how well they have learned it.

Good assessment also is fundamental to the academic success of our children for another reason: Teachers who know how to share with students just the right kinds of assessment results to help them see their progress in relation to the teacher's expectations help students take responsibility for their own success. They help them set their own markers and begin to understand what it means to grow and achieve. ("Oh, I get it, I should add more specific examples in this persuasive letter!" "Hmmm, if I included some of my own photographs and recorded observations, this science project might make a better impression.") Students cannot successfully shape their own learning priorities and study habits or make the proper effort unless they receive reliable feedback about what is working and what isn't.

A careful look at the assessment practices at your child's school can be the best consumer tool you have. The presence or absence of sound assessment practices may ultimately reveal the proof of "quality" in a classroom, school, or system. This guide is intended to help you as parents to become advocates on behalf of the well-being of your children, as patrons of and advocates for your local schools. You don't need to become an assessment expert,

"Assessment completes the contract between families and their schools."

but you do need some basic information so that you can ask the right questions and help solve problems.

Why is assessment so important?

To find out why assessment is important, we begin with a look into the classroom. Schools are only as good as the interactions that occur between teachers and students. We entrust teachers with a precious responsibility. We count on them to use their training, knowledge, and art to make sophisticated judgments about what to teach and how to teach it. This process is complicated, and it will help us to use a familiar analogy to understand the dynamics of careful instructional planning.

Imagine that you are preparing to embark on a driving trip in unfamiliar territory. Naturally, you will want an accurate map of the region. You first need to determine your final destination. Then, using the map, you figure the best route to get there. Daily mileage averages, best stopping points, and sites of interest are all important planning considerations, too. With some careful planning, you have a good chance of organizing a successful trip.

Now, in contrast to this thoughtful approach, imagine that you take off on a similar journey, but you have no map or destination, and just plan to drive for a certain length of time. Your trip will consist only of hours of unpredictable and aimless driving. Although you may encounter some points of interest, there is also the possibility you will drive into desolate back country without adequate services or accommodations.

This example, although somewhat simplistic, reveals how a teacher who does not implement sound assessment basics may run the same risks as you do when driving without a map. First, teachers needs to focus on their essential learning targets (the destination on the map): their students' learning goals. With these targets clearly in sight, it is then easier to plan backwards. Designing their own map routes, teachers must ensure that sufficient checkpoints occur along the way to know that learning is unfolding as it should.

Teachers will also want their students, in essence their copilots, to be in the car and aware of the target as well. Just as a careful driver will watch for mileage markers and road signs, an experienced teacher will also build in ways to collect data about student performance. Do my students know where they're headed? Are they still on the path? Have they taken a detour? Have they encountered some kind of road hazard?

This type of careful planning reveals the essential components of good instruction and sound assessment: a clear set of achievement expectations and a sense of how students can reach them. If the expected result is clear and the path is carefully laid out, then classroom assessment results should tell both teacher and student where to modify instruction or study tactics if necessary to get to the goal. The process also should reveal when students have veered off course and when they have succeeded.

How does quality assessment affect your child's future?

Let's leave the classroom for a moment and move to a setting more familiar to most parents — the workplace. Naturally, when we parents are concerned about our second grader's reading program or the vocational course offerings for our high school sophomore, we are thinking ahead to the ultimate impact of this education. Are my children going to be happy and successful when they are out on their own? Will the quality of their school experience today increase the odds of this occurring tomorrow? Such questions should also invite you to examine changing demands in the employment sector. As these demands increase, they require more sophisticated assessment practices in all preparatory schools. For most, this special link between school and work should come as no surprise.

Most of us already work in environments where flexibility, constant training, teamwork expectations, production targets, and rapid learning curves are the norm. With most adults now expecting to make four to six significant job changes in their professional careers, individuals without a strong skill repertoire are at a distinct disadvantage. When students exit our schools they need to possess a solid foundation of reading, writing, mathematical, and problem-solving competencies. No longer is it enough to occupy a seat in a classroom, regurgitating the minimum necessary to pass. Students coming out of this learning environment face a tough future after high school. They simply will not have the tools necessary to advance in a competitive work world where accessing, analyzing, and applying information in a new context are essential skills.

As we stated before, many educators agree about the basic building blocks necessary for world-class learning: Schools today must offer students (1) classrooms that respond rapidly to student needs, (2) more sophisticated, tightly organized learning experiences with clear and important achievement targets, and (3) sound, ongoing assessments. Students should be repeatedly asked to show what they know and can do — using rigorous

"Accessing, analyzing, and applying information . . . are essential skills."

standards. If the results suggest a lack of learning, the system must be set up to analyze the students' needs and to intervene with a reliable remedy. Teachers must be ready to modify teaching if it's obvious that their targets are unclear or haven't been met. Sounds simple, doesn't it? These conditions will not exist, however, until communities of educators and parents join in a mutual campaign to set high academic standards and promote the development and use of quality assessment practices.

Although the prescription does seem clear and workable, it has been difficult to apply consistently on a large scale. Some of the reasons for this are justified and some are inexcusable. Later in this guide we will examine these inhibiting factors in depth so that you can feel more informed as you work with your own local educators. For the moment, however, consider again that most important dynamic of all — the relationship between the classroom teacher and the student.

Are educators prepared to assess student achievement accurately?

The answer to this question may surprise you. Recent national opinion polls show that most parents trust and respect their child's teacher. This comes from real-life experience. Every day, from their own kids, they see and hear indisputable evidence defining a certain teacher as a hard-working and caring individual. Along with this respect and confidence comes an assumption that most teachers must be assessing student achievement carefully and accurately. Most believe that teachers know who is learning and who is not. Surely most parents believe that teachers are thoroughly trained to assess that achievement in the most

"Educators and parents [must] join in a mutual campaign to set high standards and promote quality assessment."

effective and efficient way. After all, this is the key part of the teacher's job! It also seems logical that any teacher not meeting standards of professional practice in their assessment of student achievement would be discovered by supervisors. And naturally these principals or administrators would have helped these teachers overcome any problems with accurate assessment. This is their job as supervisors, is it not?

As it turns out, however, these assumptions are not valid in many schools. In some classrooms, even good teachers may not be as clear as they should be about their achievement expectations. Instead, they may be more concerned with and very good at providing stimulating activities — but that lead to where? Similarly, teachers at particular grade levels within a school building or district (1) may not share a collective understanding of clear and essential learning goals or how to assess accurately, or (2) may have no idea what teachers at other grade levels are emphasizing or how they are assessing. This results not because most teachers don't care or aren't competent, but because they are not trained to define their expectations in accurately assessable ways. These same teachers may have no place to turn for help, because the vast majority of their supervising principals also are untrained in methods of sound assessment.

"Teachers may not share a collective understanding of essential learning goals."

As difficult as this may be to believe, when numerous research studies related to classroom assessment asked teachers if they think of themselves as competent, confident assessors of student achievement, the vast majority answered that they do not but would welcome whatever help they could get. These teachers have not been trained by colleges of education to fulfill these assessment responsibilities. To reach the goals of higher standards and quality assessment, we must thoughtfully examine some of the barriers and challenges to sound practice that exist in our society and school culture today. We begin by helping you look for evidence of key elements of quality assessment in your own community schools:

1. Does your school district have clear achievement expectations mapped out across all grade levels in a manner that permits students to progress continuously?

2. Does your child's teacher know and understand which of those achievement targets are her or his instructional responsibility and how those targets fit into the big picture?

3. Is your child's teacher developing and using high-quality assessments?

4. Is the teacher using assessment as a source of positive motivation to help students push for excellence?

While this guide will help you find answers to these questions, it does not show you how to fix all potential problems you may uncover. It is not our intent to have you become the problem solver in this case. Fixing curriculum or assessment problems are often technical matters requiring sophisticated professional expertise. It is our hope that you will bring any problems to the attention of the proper persons, and that you will support and assist local teachers and administrators as they seek remedies.

In the following chapters, we will take you step by step through an easy-to-understand explanation of assessment terms and practices. We provide you with practical examples, helping you to understand the teacher's classroom assessment challenge.

We want this guide to be a tool to help you, the concerned parent, support your child's school. The contents should be equally valuable for both parents and educators who want to work together on this important topic.

Before we continue, let's consider a counterpoint to the stories at the beginning of this chapter. The following vignette indicates the type of positive experiences students can and should have in school. It also sets the stage for the possibilities that can exist if parents, teachers, and administrators work together to improve the learning process.

Elliot is a junior at Austen High School. He's nearing the end of the year, and is thinking about Mrs. Powell's third-period class. This class, which addresses both American literature and American history, is one of the best experiences he's had in school. He's trying to figure out why.

Certainly, he reflects, one of the reasons is Mrs. Powell herself. She's smart, funny, and really knows her stuff. But he's had other teachers with similar talents, so there must be something else. After thinking it through, he finally decides it's the way she structures her class — especially her use of assignments, projects, and grading. For example, Mrs. Powell makes it very clear to her students (and also to their parents at open house) just what topics, skills, and goals the class will explore.

The targets for her instruction are not a mystery to anyone. In fact, in many cases she encourages the class to help her clarify her expectations. This is certainly true with writing assignments. The class spends a lot of time analyzing various writing models and isolating particular techniques that make writing effective. Sometimes Mrs. Powell uses actual student examples, other times she borrows passages from the literature they are studying. Once the students begin to under-stand the specifics, she encourages them to use the identified criteria to evaluate their own and each other's work.

Elliot also realizes that Mrs. Powell uses lots of different ways to evaluate how her students are performing. Oh, sure, there are the typical tests and papers where good, old-fashioned research and memori-zation are important. But he also thinks about the projects everyone completes where you can pick an area of interest and really go after it. These projects have lots of different parts: research, writing, pre-sentations, computer work, and even art connections. Once again, the class discusses ahead of time the standards for quality work, and students are able to visualize the level of excellence they wish to achieve.

He realizes that he's also very involved when it comes to keeping his working portfolio. He gets to choose many of the pieces to include in his final portfolio — some represent examples of his best work, some are pieces he's chosen to redo and improve, some even show difficulties he's encountered. The key, he decides, is the fact that in almost all of these examples, he is really plugged into the whole grading process. He understands what's expected, he's invited to help set certain stan-dards, and he is allowed to tailor parts of his work to his own needs and interests.

It's funny, Elliot realizes, but when he's monitoring his own progress he works harder and pushes himself farther than any teacher could. Besides the personal satisfaction, he knows it's probably good prepa-ration for college. After Mrs. Powell's class, he's feeling a lot more confident about his academic success once he graduates from high school. He's ready for a break but is feeling good about the work he's completed this term.

How does assessment fit into the classroom?

If we wish to ensure that our children's classroom experiences and assessments really promote learning, there are a few important things we need to understand. For instance, we need to understand that since we were in school, some aspects of schooling have remained the same and others have changed. The same is true of student achievement expectations. And while sometimes teachers motivate children in the same ways our teachers motivated us, often they use more effective ways.

Most of today's teachers also assess student achievement using the same methods our teachers used, but often there are important differences here, too. And finally, some teachers use some traditional ways to communicate about student achievement, like report card grades, while some have supplemented these with more innovative means of communicating, like portfolios.

As a result, we can't judge what's happening in today's schools solely on the basis of our own experience. We must invest some time and effort to understand why schools are changing and be productive partners in managing those changes. So, let's explore how our assessment traditions and more recent innovations are playing out in schools.

15

How do effective schools work?

Essentially, "good" schools are still like they were when we were in school, with a few important exceptions.

Consistencies with the past

Schools function most effectively when all of the following are true:

- School and community define a successful school as one that produces the greatest possible achievement among the largest possible proportion of its student population.

- Educators and communities collaborate in defining what students should learn to become competent adults.

- Teachers care about and are able to influence how well their students are learning.

- Teachers are masters of the subjects they expect their students to learn.

- Teachers know when and how to use effective instruction to help students learn.

- Students are motivated to invest the time and mental energy to try to learn.

- Schools provide students and their families with clear feedback about specific academic abilities attained and not yet attained.

These are universals. They applied to schools when we were young, apply to schools of today, and will apply to the schools our grandchildren attend.

The first entry on the list deserves some additional comment. We live in a society in which citizens hold profoundly differing views about what an "effective" school is and does. Some parents merely hope their schools can be physically safe places for their children. Others want their schools to be places in which students can "self-actualize," or learn to make their own way — to take charge of their lives. Still others contend that we live in a competitive society and want winners and losers — good schools that sort students from the highest to the lowest achievers. And then there are those who contend that schools must maximize achievement for the largest possible proportion of the students to be considered successful.

To be sure, these are not mutually exclusive. Students certainly can self-actualize in a safe, competitive environment where everyone's achievement is encouraged. But we should not consider a school a success simply because it's students are ranked in order of achievement. You must determine whether the academic standards used are sufficiently high to warrant use of the ranking system in the first place. Students who are highly ranked within a generally low-achieving group are not successful, regardless of how self-fulfilled those students are.

It can be difficult for schools and communities to build into their programs all of the elements needed to attain high levels of academic achievement. Shifting political forces, differences of parental opinion, often declining resources, a lack of sufficient training, difficult labor relations — these and other forces can conspire to block our path to truly effective schools. But still educators strive for excellence, constantly learning new lessons themselves and trying to improve student achievement.

"Citizens hold profoundly differing views about what an 'effective' school is."

Recent improvements

In other ways, schools are different today from when we were in school. Many of the changes portend good things for our children. For example, we have a far clearer sense today than ever before of what it means for students to succeed academically in school — to become

- *Proficient readers* — Psychologists have helped us to more clearly understand the cognitive basis of reading comprehension.

- *Effective writers* — Authors have explained the writing process and standards of effective writing in greater detail.

- *Skilled math problem solvers* — Mathematicians have defined the processes of mathematical reasoning with greater clarity.

- *Masters of the natural or social sciences* — Scientists have defined in sharp detail several different, yet productive, ways to use science effectively.

- *Proficient in foreign languages* — Graduated levels of oral and written communication have been clearly and completely defined.

"Well-defined targets provide an excellent basis for more effective teaching."

These and other well-defined targets provide an excellent basis for more effective teaching and quality assessment today than ever before.

In addition, we know far more today about how the learning brain works. We know how to adjust instruction to meet specific student needs. We more completely understand principles of student motivation. And, we also understand more clearly how assessment fits into the schooling equation.

For example, we used to think that instruction worked best when we taught first and then tested afterwards. Now we understand that assessment contributes more to promoting maximum student achievement when we assess *while* students are learning — not just at the end.

We also believed that the best way to promote learning was to pound knowledge into students' heads via rote memorization and then have them regurgitate it back on a test. We know now that this strategy can leave students knowing a great deal but understanding little of it, rendering them unable to apply the material. The consequences of such inadequate learning often emerge in college or adult life, where success is contingent on having understood the principles underlying learned material. We now define sound practices as those that promote understanding and application *while the material is being learned.*

We used to think the best way to motivate all students was to promise rewards of high grades for those who scored high and to threaten low grades for those who did not. We now understand through decades of research that this works for some students but not for all. Unfortunately, it can encourage students to focus on immediate performance as reflected in the grade received rather than on the actual achievement (knowledge and understanding) that forms the basis of later success. When students are taught to value short-term results only, those grades become lights so brilliant that they blind students to what the grades are supposed to represent. This can leave even our most successful students feeling that reading or writing, for example, are not worth doing in their own right; that such activities are without value beyond the grades they generate. The result can

"Assessment contributes more to . . . student achievement when we assess while students are learning."

be a kind of dependence on the reward giver that stifles risk taking and creativity. We see this when high school students (such as Mike in the opening vignette in Chapter 1) opt for easy courses rather than more challenging ones merely to maintain high grade point averages or when they misrepresent their own learning through cheating. These practices promote the appearance of a high level of performance but have devastating consequences for students' actual achievement and long-term success.

We now understand that motivating students is a complex enterprise. Sometimes we must supplement reward and punishment systems with motivators that, for example, encourage students to learn to read and write because they sense the contributions these activities will make to the quality of their lives or to their potential for success in school.

So, the bottom line is that schools still work in many ways as they did when we were in school. But as our understanding of learning and schooling has evolved and as it continues to evolve, we must be ready to take advantage of new insights about the roles assessment can play in maximizing our children's achievement.

How does assessment work in school?

"When we assess, . . . we gather information about how much students have learned."

When we assess how well students are doing, we gather information about how much those students have learned. Teachers do this using tests, quizzes, homework assignments, projects, interactions with students during instruction, and so on. In school, assessments work in many ways, serving many purposes, reflecting many different kinds of student achievement, and relying on many different methods. But to work effectively, all assessments must be of very high quality; that is, they must accurately reflect expectations and provide enough information to lead to dependable conclusions. Assessment results inform many decision makers and answer many questions that bear directly on the quality of the schooling experience for your children.

To understand the implications of this, let's explore the various purposes, kinds of achievement, and methods that can contribute to the quality of student assessments.

Why we assess

We assess student achievement in schools for many reasons. That is, assessment results serve many different users in many different ways. As parents, we have a tendency to think that teachers assess merely to assign report card grades. While this is certainly true, it is by no means the only or perhaps even the most important use of assessment. Let's consider others.

Teachers use such day-to-day classroom assessment results as performance on homework, chapter tests, unit tests, and special class projects to answer questions such as the following:

Is my instruction working for the class as a whole?
For which students is it working or not working?
Do I need to go over the material again to ensure learning?
Which students need special attention?
What special attention do they need?
How should I group students to promote maximum learning?
What grades should I assign on report cards?

As *parents*, we use the assessment results that our children bring home to tell us the following:

> *Are my children succeeding in school?*
> *Does that success extend to all subjects?*
> *Do my children need special help?*
> *How can I motivate my children to study hard and succeed?*
> *Do we need to adjust our home environment somehow?*
> *Are my children's teachers doing an effective job?*
> *Do we have a good school in our neighborhood?*
> *How can I do a better job to support my children's learning?*

But the list of users and uses of assessment results doesn't stop here. It also includes *students*. We rarely think of students as users of assessment results. We tend to cast them in a passive role. Teachers use the results, as do parents. But students? Yes — right from the very moment they start school! They almost immediately tune into their teacher's evaluations of their work to tell them if they are succeeding, to see if their efforts are paying off, and to see if their teachers think they can do it. Based on their impressions of these matters — that is, *their own personal interpretations* of assessment results — our children begin to set their own internal academic expectations. But more importantly, they begin to decide if they have any hope of success in the future. Depending on their conclusion, they decide whether future academic challenges are worth trying. And since level of effort connects directly to level of academic success, these are profoundly important decisions on the student's part.

This is precisely why we can no longer think of assessment merely as something attached onto the end of teaching — as a test at the end of a unit or a grade at the end of a semester, as it

"Our children [must] begin to set their own internal academic expectations."

was for most of us when we were in school. (Of course, it shouldn't have been so *then*, either!) If that's when assessment happens and the results indicate a student's lack of success, it may be too late to do anything about it. And if the material not learned is prerequisite to later material, this may doom the student to future failure, too.

But parents, teachers, and students are not the only important assessment users. While perhaps not as immediately important for student success, others do need access to accurate information about student achievement to do their jobs well. For example, the school building *principal* examines assessment results summarized across all classrooms to see if the school's instructional program is working effectively. The *guidance counselor* or *school psychologist* uses assessment results to help students and their families cope or make educational or vocational decisions. District *curriculum planners* must study assessment results summarized across school buildings to see whether the districtwide program of instruction is effective.

We also must consider the decisions made by *superintendents* and *school boards* at the district level. They evaluate student performance information to set policy and allocate education funds in ways that ensure quality schools. Similarly, *state departments of education* and *state or federal legislators* establish education laws, policies, and regulations, accredit schools, allocate state resources, and set educational program priorities based in part on patterns of student achievement. Finally, *potential employers* also need accurate academic job-related information about applicants.

Clearly, assessment — the process of gathering information about student achievement — weaves itself deeply into the fabric of schooling. If all of the classroom, school, community, district, state, and federal assessment users identified here have access to accurate information about student achievement arising from quality assessments, then they will make sound decisions and students will be well served.

Imagine the plight of the child trying to succeed in a classroom, school, or district in which all these various assessment users cannot count on quality assessments to provide accurate information about student achievement. Teachers could misdiagnose students' learning needs or assign incorrect grades, students would feel they had failed when in fact they had succeeded at learning, parents would assume all is well when it is not, principals would label effective teachers ineffective, and so on. For these reasons, we contend that quality assessments lie at the heart of effective schools and the academic well-being of our children. We cannot overemphasize their importance.

What we assess

As we prepare for the twenty-first century, educators face the challenge of assessing an increasingly broader range of different kinds of student achievement, including all of the proficiencies our generation had to master plus many more.

First, as always, students must master (that is, know and understand) the *subject matter content* of such disciplines as science, technology, and social studies in an increasingly complex world, math facts and concepts, and information derived from literature, among other content areas. But they face one challenge that many of their parents didn't face in school.

Most of today's adults went to schools where we were considered masters of content when we had learned it outright — when we could retrieve it from memory when we needed it. However, in today's information age, our children face the challenge of dealing with two ways of knowing. They must not only *know* a great deal outright, but must also be skilled at *retrieving* a great deal of additional information using reference materials, computer databases, and other sources. They must learn to be information managers, not just information memorizers.

In addition, knowing it, knowing where to find it, and understanding it are not even enough. Our children need to be able to use their knowledge and understanding to *reason and solve practical problems*. They must become critical thinkers, comparative reasoners, analytical thinkers, and users of the scientific method. They must learn principles, not simply acquire information. And even more importantly, before they leave school, they need to be ready to monitor the quality of their own reasoning. Everyday family life and the workplace both demand sound thinkers able to solve complex problems.

But the targets our children must hit don't stop here — knowing and reasoning are not even enough today. In addition, they must learn certain *performance skills* — where it's the doing that is important. They must learn to read aloud fluently, speak articulately (perhaps in multiple languages), perform physical skills, work cooperatively as part of a team, and so on. And beyond these, sometimes we ask students to use their knowledge, reasoning prowess, and skills to create *products* that meet certain standards of quality — like writing research papers, building models, setting up science fair exhibits, and creating art or craft products.

Knowing, reasoning, being skillful, creating products — all are critically important ways of achieving in school. To know the words in the Gettysburg Address but not to understand them is not good enough. If we assess only the former, we cannot know if the examinee understands.

To know and even to understand the steps in long division is not enough if students can't apply that mathematical knowledge to reason through real-life problems. We assess productively when we assess *both* knowledge *and* reasoning.

Further, it is not enough even to know and reason well if students fail to master the skills needed to perform experiments in science, speak proficiently in English or foreign language class, or contribute to a team effort. Teachers must assess performance skills to see if students have mastered them.

And finally, it is not sufficient to know, to reason, and to master skills if students cannot assemble all the pieces into quality products when called for. Real life expects high-quality results. To determine if students can create products that meet life's standards of quality, teachers must help them learn those standards, create products, and evaluate performance in terms of the agreed upon standards.

The essential foundations of effective schools are (1) clear knowledge, reasoning, skill and product targets that are (2) carefully integrated across grade levels, and (3) teachers who are themselves confident, competent masters of the targets their students are to master.

Imagine the plight of students studying in classrooms where the valued achievement expectations have not been spelled out or, even more seriously, have not been mastered by the teachers who are to teach them. Imagine the problems that might arise if your child's teacher was unable to accurately assess mastery of content, reasoning proficiency, skills, or product development capabilities. Under these circumstances, clearly even the most able students would have difficulty succeeding academically. Teachers would have great difficulty planning instruction around achievement expectations they themselves did not understand, and their assessments would likely misrepresent actual student achievement. Consider the implications of such a scenario for student motivation. How many times does a student have to work hard to learn something, succeed in learning it at a very high level, and still score low on a poorly constructed test before that student concludes that he or she is incapable of learning or that studying hard is just not worth it?

Remember Lily, the dejected student we met at the beginning of Chapter One? Suppose Lily's teacher had really examined her curriculum to be sure it emphasized knowing, reasoning, applying skills, creating quality products, or some combination of these. And suppose, with some good training, this teacher was also able to implement a sound plan to assess these different ways of achieving. Under this scenario, Lily's report card grades would have been a function of how much she had learned. But imagine for this example that her final grades were a mixed bag — mostly A's, but a few B's and even a C. Lily might still have been frustrated because her grades were not up to her usual stellar standards, but there would have been one big difference.

In this revised context, Lily also would have understood why she received these grades. Her marks would have been directly tied back to performances and assignments driven by a tight curriculum with clear objectives. In addition, Lily would have had a variety of opportunities to display her knowledge and reasoning using different types of application possibilities. Finally, as each assignment or test or project or presentation occurred, expectations would have been clear and grading guidelines established and explained to students in advance.

It's interesting to think how Lily's conversation with her dad might have changed in this situation. Some of their conversation may have focused on dissatisfaction and a desire to do better. But this theme would more than likely focus on Lily — not the classroom and the teacher. An informed Lily would know how the grades came to be and she would also know what would need to change if straight A's were her target for the next round!

How we assess

What strategies do educators use to find out if students are learning, given all of these kinds of achievement to assess, and given all of the people who rely on assessment results to help them do their job? We assess in many different ways.

When we were growing up, our teachers relied heavily on *tests that had right answers*. Remember? They used multiple-choice tests, true/false tests, and matching and short answer fill-in questions. It's the same today. These remain viable options.

But our teachers were not limited to them. They also used *essay tests*. In addition, they observed and judged us as we performed,

"What strategies do educators use to find out if students are learning?"

as in speech class, music competitions, and delivering Shakespeare or Walt Whitman poems, familiar demonstrations of achievement that today are termed *performance assessments*.

And finally, in some cases, our teachers gathered information about our achievement through *direct interaction* — by talking with us, as in class discussions and oral exams. Teachers continue to use all these methods today.

We see frequent reference to assessment "reform" in the media these days. This leads many to believe that sweeping changes are underway in how schools test their students. Please understand that this is not the case. Educators are not inventing new methods of evaluating students. The four methods listed have been around and in use in schools for decades. But what *is* changing over time is the *manner* in which educators apply these options. We are seeing less reliance on right answer tests alone and greater reliance on essay and performance assessments.

The reason for this change is that we now understand with greater clarity the extreme complexity of the achievement targets students are expected to meet. While some still can be translated into multiple-choice tests, many cannot. To assess oral reading, speaking, or writing proficiency, to mention just a few examples, we must have students actually perform so teachers can observe and evaluate proficiency. We need performance assessments for these. To see if our students can solve complex problems, we must pose such problems and evaluate their success. Often this requires an essay or performance test.

Another aspect of assessment that is not changing is the levels at which educators assess. When we were in school, obviously, we completed many classroom assessments and, in addition, we took periodic standardized tests. Both remain important today. However, students currently face more standardized tests than we did, with district, state, national, and even international assessments in place in many schools.

This means teachers need to know when to use each method and how to use each well. In this context, it is relevant to ask: Did our teachers know how to use all of these methods well to accurately assess our achievement when we were in school? Are today's teachers prepared to assess the achievement of our children accurately using all of these methods?

How to assess well

If we parents are to ask informed questions about assessment practices in our schools, we must understand what it means to accurately evaluate student achievement. It is not enough merely to know what kinds of achievement teachers assess (knowledge, reasoning, skills, or products). Nor is it sufficient that we understand the methods they might use (right answer, essay, performance or interactive assessment). In addition, we must understand how these parts fit together.

A quality assessment provides a clear, accurate, and timely picture of what a student has learned, while at the same time spelling out which achievement expectations have not yet been met.

For example, what method would a teacher use who wanted to determine whether students have mastered some required science knowledge? One excellent choice is to ask questions and see if students can answer them correctly. To do this, the teacher can rely on right answer tests (multiple-choice, true/false, etc.), essay tests, or interactive assessments. Since students wouldn't be required to demonstrate anything, performance tests aren't a good choice here.

As parents, we might want to be sure our child's teacher has determined in advance precisely what knowledge our child is to understand. While we may not be able to judge its appropriateness, we *can* evaluate the presence or absence of such expectations. And when assessing this kind of achievement, we might expect the teacher to be confident about what kinds of methods to use.

To assess if students can use their knowledge to figure things out (that is, to reason and solve problems), teachers can rely on right answer, essay, or performance tests, as well as on interaction with students. But to use any of these well, teachers must begin with a clear sense of the kinds of reasoning to be demonstrated. Do they expect analytical thinking (figuring out how parts work together), comparative thinking (how things are alike or different), or critical thinking (defending an opinion)? Further, the teacher must be skilled in developing assessments that ask students to reason.

To assess mastery of performance skills or product development capabilities, where successfully giving the speech, writing the term paper, creating the science fair exhibit, or playing the musical instrument is the criteria for proficiency, teachers must rely on performance assessments. Multiple-choice or essay tests simply won't work here. They must actually see students performing enough times or examine enough of a child's products to be able to make dependable judgments about their achievement.

"[Teachers] must actually see students performing enough . . . to make dependable judgments."

As parents, we should expect to see evidence that these kinds of performance skills and product targets are considered important in the classroom. That is, when they are relevant, teachers should be able to show us examples of such expectations. Further, we should see teachers relying on observation and judgment of actual performance when assessing student mastery of these targets.

Table 2.1 summarizes the ways your child's teacher can use assessment methods to reflect different kinds of learning. But to make any of them work well, each teacher must start the process with a complete picture of what students are to learn and with a refined knowledge of when and how to use each assessment method to determine when they have learned it. Only then can the achievement targets and assessment methods be married in sound and appropriate ways.

Table 2.1 Which assessment method works best?

TO ASSESS IF THE STUDENT	"RIGHT ANSWER" TEST	ESSAY TEST	PERFORMANCE ASSESSMENT	DIRECT CONVERSATION
Has mastered content knowledge	Good match	Good match	Not the best match	Good match
Can use knowledge to solve problems	Good match for some problems	Good match for some problems	Good match for some problems	Good match for some problems
Can demonstrate performance skills	Not a good match	Not a good match	Good match	Good for communication skills only
Can use skills to create products	Not a good match	Not a good match	Good match	Not a good match

But merely selecting the appropriate assessment method is only part of the teacher's challenge. Once they select a method, teachers must know how to use it in a manner that results in enough accurate information about student achievement to avoid mismeasuring that achievement. They must understand how to collect samples of student work and how to evaluate them in a bias-free manner.

To sample student achievement well, the teacher must ask enough questions to be sure to cover the material. To avoid bias, she or he must understand where test bias can come from — what can go wrong during the testing process — and how to prevent these problems. For example, what if the test covers four chapters in the text, but most of the test items focus on only two chapters? Such a test would fail to represent the material fairly — it would be *biased* in its coverage.

Or, what if a student has, in fact, mastered the material covered on the multiple-choice test but cannot read well enough to comprehend the test items? If that student scores low, the teacher might conclude incorrectly that the student failed to learn. The same problem can occur when a nonwriter is faced with an essay assessment or a non-English speaker must complete a test written in English. The result can be incorrect conclusions about student mastery of the required material. These are sources of biased (inaccurate) results.

Or, what if a performance assessment in physical education places a premium on strength? Such a test might be biased against students of slight build. An assessment is considered *biased* when students' scores are influenced by factors unrelated to the kind of achievement being assessed. Such assessments unfairly place some students at a systematic advantage or disadvantage. All teachers and administrators must know when and how to guard against such problems.

Let's consider an example

To understand how achievement targets and assessment methods come together, recall what happened when you were ready to get your driver's license. What does a person need to know and understand to be a competent safe driver? The answer includes the essential parts of a car and how they work, rules of the road, meaning of road signs, and so on. How did the license bureau assess your mastery of this prerequisite knowledge and understanding? Right: the multiple-choice test!

What kinds of reasoning are required to drive effectively? As circumstances unfold before you on the road, you must be able to interpret them accurately and figure out what to do next. How did they assess this? While you may not explicitly recall, the multiple-choice "written test" presented some such situations, and you had to pick the correct action (the right answer).

But remember how other such sets of circumstances unfolded before your very eyes during the road test? Ah, the road test . . . now there's an experience few forget: starting the car, pulling into traffic, using turn signals (and for the older of us, hand signals!), parallel parking, and so on. These represent the important performance skills of driving. When it comes to driving, one can know all the right answers and still not be able to perform as skillfully as necessary. The license bureau sampled your performance on the road to see if you could put your knowledge and understanding into action. It was the *combination* of written test and performance assessment that told the examiners if you had mastered knowledge, reasoning, and skills to a sufficient degree that you were ready to be certified as a safe driver. Either assessment by itself would have been inadequate.

It is just the same in the classroom. Students must master prerequisite knowledge, reasoning proficiencies, performance skills, and product development capabilities to be judged ready to be good readers, writers, math problem solvers, or masters of the natural or social sciences. And just as with the examination to certify readiness to drive safely, teachers must be ready to turn to multiple forms of assessment to get at the real keys to academic success. They can use right answer and essay tests to see if students have mastered prerequisite knowledge, and use performance assessments to see if they have become skillful.

How to communicate effectively about student achievement

Remember in Chapter 1 when we spoke of teachers needing a clear map of where students are going and how they'll get there? Such a map permits travelers to check progress along the way to be sure they are on course. When the "destination" is a certain kind of achievement, classroom assessments can provide teachers, students, and parents with sufficient feedback to determine if they are progressing toward ultimate success. In this case, obviously, the assessments used to track progress must provide accurate information about current achievement status. But that's not enough.

In addition, teachers must effectively communicate those results to students and parents. What are the most effective

"Teachers must effectively communicate those results to students and parents."

ways to deliver messages about student achievement? The answer depends on who the intended message receivers are and how they are likely to use the results.

Some parents like to receive their messages about academic performance in a summary form such as report card grades (A, B, C, etc.). This provides apparently easy-to-understand information about their child's achievement in relation both to the teacher's standards and to other students. But remember, grades are a basis for effective communication only when both teacher and parent or student know how each letter grade relates to how much students have achieved. More about this later.

Test scores also provide summary information about student achievement. Sometimes these are scores on the teacher's classroom quizzes or unit tests. These scores typically reflect what proportion of the required material the student has mastered. Other times, the scores arise from the annual school district standardized tests, statewide assessments, and college admissions tests. These scores typically tell how examinees performed in relation to other students who took the same test. But again remember, test scores work as the basis for effective communication only if those who interpret them understand what they mean; that is, what kinds of achievement were measured and how scores related to those expectations. Again, we will discuss this in Chapter 3.

While grades and test scores provide information usable for some decision makers, others want and need greater detail. For example, teachers receiving new students need to know from their previous teachers the newcomers' current levels of achievement in order to plan what comes next. In addition, students themselves need greater detail as they try to figure out what they are doing well and how they can improve. Prospective employers sometimes seek information about specific things students can and cannot do. In all of these cases, examples of student work, checklists of specific achievements, detailed parent-teacher conferences or narrative (written) descriptions of student achievement are far more useful than a single summary letter grade or test score, because they preserve and convey a greater level of detail about student success.

There is no single best way to deliver messages about student achievement. Grades meet some needs some of the time, but cannot hope to serve all communication purposes. Teachers need to have other means at their disposal. To meet the communication challenges of the classroom, each teacher must start with a clear sense of the valued targets, and must then transform those targets into quality assessments, build a reservoir of accurate information about each student's achievement, and be ready to deliver those results in various forms to those who need access to it.

But remember, if teachers start with poor-quality assessments and misinformation about student performance, they can't deliver an informed message no matter what communication vehicle they use. And, as importantly, they can't begin to help students see how to improve their own learning.

Summary of key insights for parents

What, then, are the key things parents need to know about the assessment process to understand how that process might affect their children's lives?

"Grades . . . cannot hope to serve all communication purposes."

First, many individuals rely on assessment results to inform decisions that bear directly on the quality of students' schooling experiences. But the *first* users of assessment results are almost always *the students themselves*. Educators and parents alike tend to frequently overlook this fact. Our children read the messages of assessment to decide whether they are capable. This is how they decide if future effort is likely to pay off. If the assessments are sound, the results accurate, and the meaning of results clear to students, then they can make good decisions. But if these assessments are unsound — if the results fail to accurately reflect their true achievement — or if students misunderstand or misinterpret those results, our children may be harmed.

Second, we must honor the information needs of all who rely on assessment results to make decisions that influence our children's academic success. The needs of only one or two groups of assessment users — whether they be teachers, parents, or policy makers — cannot drive the entire system. All who have a contribution to make are entitled to timely information about student achievement in a form they understand and can use.

Third, quality assessments must arise from a sharply focused set of achievement expectations. Teachers must know and understand precisely what content, reasoning, skills, and products students are to master. Only teachers who are themselves masters of the content their students are to master can ensure accurate assessment and thus student well-being.

Fourth, our broadening range of achievement expectations requires — does not simply permit — the use of a variety of assessment methods. One method — say, the multiple-choice test — cannot hope to cover all of the kinds of achievement teachers expect of their students. This reality carries with it the requirement that each teacher knows what method to use when, and the expectation that teachers know and understand how to use each method to sample achievement appropriately and in a bias-free way.

Finally, effective communication requires that the message sender (most often the teacher) and message receivers agree on what is being said. What does a report card grade of B mean in terms of actual student learning? What does it say about which achievement expectations are being met and which are not? When we agree on those expectations and on the meaning of the symbols we use to communicate, we lay a strong foundation for effective communication.

In the next chapter, we explore the extent to which educators are prepared to meet these standards of quality assessment and effective communication.

What should we see behind the classroom door?

Thus far, we have discussed why a quality assessment system is such an important ingredient in good schools and have defined specific standards of high-quality assessment. Clearly, both traditional and innovative assessment practices, as well as classroom assessments and standardized tests, have contributions to make — when used in balanced, thoughtful ways by qualified users.

Now let's begin to apply some of these lessons. In this chapter we will examine how teachers can weave good teaching and sound assessment seamlessly into their classroom environments. In the process, we will alert you to problems or gaps that may exist when assessment is handled ineffectively in the classroom. After reading this chapter, you will be a more effective partner with your child's teacher in promoting the effective use of quality assessments.

The standards of quality assessment

As you will recall, we have framed five standards of high-quality assessment.

1. Clear targets

The targets of instruction — the teacher's achievement expectations — must be clear and appropriate. Without a clear sense of what we are assessing, how can we assess it well? A teacher must be able to define the specific achievement the assessment is to reflect.

2. Clear purposes for assessing

The reason we measure achievement must be clear and appropriate. Teachers must begin their assessment design with a clear sense of who will use the results and how. Without a sense of whose information needs are to be served, quality assessment will remain out of reach.

3. Appropriate assessment methods

Educators have a variety of methods at their disposal to create a good match between the desired target and the assessment method used. No single method can accurately reflect all kinds of achievement. Therefore, teachers must select and develop proper methods for the context. They get to choose, but along with this freedom comes the responsibility to choose well.

4. Appropriate sampling of student achievement

Any test is composed of only a sample of all the test items a teacher could have posed if testing time were unlimited. Obviously, however, time is never unlimited. So teachers must use testing time wisely. They must gather the best available information with minimum time investment.

5. Elimination of bias and distortion

Teachers must think in advance about how to control for possible sources of outside interference that may invalidate assessment results, which can be numerous and challenging to overcome. Problems can arise from among students themselves, from within the test questions, and from within the testing environment in the classroom. If teachers fail to account for them, they risk collecting inaccurate information.

What can you look for?

Keeping these standards in mind, then, let's explore what can go right and what can go wrong in the assessment process in your child's classroom. We offer a set of criteria you can apply in evaluating each standard. *If you sense that something might be wrong, you need to voice concern diplomatically, by having a conversation with the teacher or speaking with the principal.* Point out to those in authority precisely why you are concerned. In Chapter 4, we offer specific suggestions about how to do this.

Clear and appropriate targets

It's a good idea here to remember the road map analogy from Chapter 1. Good teachers are precise about what they want their students to learn. They always have a clear picture in mind of their end learning goal(s), and they also break this larger objective down into smaller pieces, the step-by-step road map leading to the target. In addition, they will be crystal clear about their place in the big picture of long-term student success. For example, a primary-grade teacher will understand how the beginning writing proficiencies students are learning relate to more advanced skills expected during elementary grades. Middle school teachers will see the links between math skills they teach and high school expectations.

Remember, though, without a written curriculum formalizing what is important to teach, it is impossible to develop valid assessments. Depending on a school district's size and resources, this curriculum may be simple or elaborate. When it comes to determining the basis of classroom assessment, however, the size and packaging of the district's version of achievement expectations are not as important as the teacher's ability to demonstrate understanding of the essential instructional goals required in her or his classroom. You may not understand all that they say, especially as your child advances to technical topics or to the upper grades of high school. But you *should* see an enthusiastic teacher confidently describing what it means to succeed in that classroom.

As you listen to or read their description, tune into several keys. If your child is expected to master content, can the teacher specify *what* content? Look for a written outline of content priorities. If effective reasoning and problem solving is expected, precisely *what* kinds of reasoning? Are students expected to demonstrate performance skills? What ones? Are they to create products? To meet what specific quality standards? Teachers who are focused in these ways are prepared to assess well.

From another perspective, listen for a sense of integration of achievement expectations over the span of the school year, across different grade levels, and among different classrooms in the same school or district. Does your child's teacher seem to know how new material relates to what has come before? To what is to follow? Does the teacher have a sense of long-term achievement expectations? Have teachers from your school or district helped to establish the targets your child is to hit? Teachers who possess a broad view of integrated learning are in a position to assess well.

"Do your children know what is expected?"

And finally, listen to your children to see if achievement expectations are clear to them. There should be no mysteries regarding the meaning of success. Do your children know what is expected? This does not simply mean that they know what assignments are due when. It means they know how to make sure each assignment is done well. Has the teacher shared this vision, along with a vocabulary that lets your children in on the secrets to success? When students can see the map, they can track their own progress and take partial responsibility for their own academic success. When you can't sense where you are headed, it's hard to feel that you could succeed if you tried. Motivation can flag. Teachers who set their students up to assess their own achievement prepare those students to take charge of their learning — a crucial lifelong skill.

Here are some of the things that can go wrong with achievement targets as the basis for classroom assessment:

- They might be missing — there might be a lack of focused expectations.

- They might not be coordinated over the year or across grade levels.

- The teacher might not be a master of the targets students are to learn.

- Students might not be aware of or understand what is expected of them.

If you ask, you may find clearly articulated and carefully coordinated expectations being effectively taught by confident, competent teachers who share their vision of success with their students. We sincerely hope you do. In the event that you do not, we suggest in the next chapter how you might help remedy the situation.

Look for activities that reflect expectations. With few exceptions, day-to-day classroom practices and activities should mesh with preestablished learning targets. Although this seems logical, such a critical link may in fact be missing.

For example, remember when you were in school, sometimes you would be so deeply involved in creating such interesting products or projects that you lost track of time. These can be among our most powerful learning experiences — but only if the activities connect directly to (promise to result in) the desired learning. Engaging in a heated discussion, completing a nifty craft project, or watching a compelling film, while motivational, are pointless wastes of valuable time if they don't help students follow the road map to academic success. Experienced teachers know their students aren't just "doing," they're "learning." As schools work harder and harder to compete for student attention in our media- and information-saturated society, it is easy to see how student involvement can become a goal unto itself. It is a hollow goal, however, unless it is coupled with a demonstrated improvement in skills.

Clear assessment purposes

If you ask teachers "Why are you testing my child? How will the results of the test be used?," they should be ready to provide commonsense, understandable answers. You should be able to tell if they already have asked themselves these same questions. Look for a range of varying uses — not just one use, such as to assign report card grades.

Naturally they will test to determine overall student performance leading to an eventual grade. But they should have other uses for their assessments. Do they use them to check for student understanding, so they know when they need to go over material again? Do they use student performance to determine the effectiveness of their teaching strategies — to see what they need to do differently the next time? Your child's teachers should be able to discuss times when assessment results have led them to change their own instruction.

In addition, listen for awareness of the fact that students are users of assessment results too, as are parents. Teachers should be able to identify specific decisions students make on the basis of their perceptions of their own success as achievers. And they should quickly bring you, the parent, into the process too, by acknowledging that families play a key decision-making role in student learning.

At the school or district level, administrators periodically assess large numbers of students with standardized tests. Ask the principal or superintendent exactly how those results are used to better your child's school. What decisions do these test results affect? Your child's teacher should know, too. Continuous school improvement requires the analysis and use of these data to inform strategic changes. Often schools can take a beating over local newspaper publications of lower-than-expected test results. However, if local policy makers are sincerely using the data to make necessary and tough changes, then those actions, rather than the scores themselves, should promise to help more students succeed.

When schools or teachers ignore this standard of clear testing purposes, then problems are likely to manifest themselves in one of two ways. First, you may find assessment happening without the assessor knowing who will use the results and how. When teachers or administrators cannot specify in advance precisely how they will use the assessment process and/or its results to help students attain higher levels of achievement — such as when it is used as a form of punishment ("Your penalty for misbehaving is twice as many items on the next test.") or as a matter of habit or tradition ("We test students at this time every year.") — a red flag should go up in your mind.

Second, you may find testing purposes defined too narrowly. For example, consider a middle school social studies teacher who administers end-of-chapter, multiple-choice quizzes only to assign grades. No attention is paid to using assessment results to diagnose student needs so instruction can be planned around those needs, to help students see themselves improve, or for practice to promote greater achievement. When assessment is for grades only, worry that instruction can march irreversibly forward with no sense of where your child is on the learning continuum. Students who see themselves as being left behind stop trying. And obviously, when they stop trying, they stop learning.

Proper assessment methods

The third standard for quality assessment asks teachers to match assessment methods appropriately to learning targets. As mentioned earlier, in recent years there has been a marked broadening in the range of methods used. For example, sometimes students might take paper and pencil multiple-choice tests, because such tests fit the targets their teachers expected them to master, such as content knowledge. But other times, teachers' expectations cannot be translated into multiple-choice or true/false test items. When the assessment is of student reasoning proficiency, often essay assessments are best. When students are also completing complex projects, giving class presentations, or collecting several samples of their products in portfolios, performance assessment is the method of choice.

If your child is in the primary grades (kindergarten through third grade), look for almost total reliance on assessments based on observation (performance assessment) and on direct personal interaction with your child. Teachers should not attempt to use right answer or paper and pencil essay tests until children have developed the prerequisite reading and writing skills.

In short, effective teachers are artists at fashioning these target–method alignments. To see if teachers are ready to do this,

"What preparation has the . . . staff had to accurately assess student achievement?"

ask them, or ask district or school administrators, this question: What preparation has the faculty and staff had to accurately assess student achievement? To use traditional or innovative assessments confidently, one must participate in appropriate training that includes extensive guided practice. There is reason to believe that, through no fault of their own, teachers in many schools may not have been given access to that training. The same holds for their supervisors. Research conducted over the past several decades reveals that fewer than half of currently practicing teachers completed any assessment coursework during training and that very few have received inservice training during their teaching careers.

You may be surprised to learn that only eleven of the fifty states currently require demonstrated competence in assessment as a condition for being licensed to teach. Only two states hold principals to rigorous assessment certification standards.

We parents should never simply assume that teachers in our schools are prepared to assess well. They may be. We do not intend to indict all teachers or administrators on this count. Many do an outstanding job. Many districts and even one whole state (Washington) have elevated professional development in assessment to the highest priority. In those cases, assessment competence is improving. We want to be sure all parents are aware that children can fall victim to inept assessment by well-meaning but ill-prepared educators.

So as an interested and supportive parent, you may want to ask about the professional training program related to assessment in your particular district. Be diplomatic in asking: Have we evaluated the current state of preparedness to assess well among our faculty? How are teachers and administrators encouraged to learn more about assessment? Are there workshops, study groups, or opportunities for shared learning among staff? If no such professional development program is currently in place, gentle but consistent suggestions may be all it will take to start the ball rolling. At the end of this guide, we offer suggested resources that you can share with your local school staff.

In summary with respect to this standard of quality, look for evidence of the use of a variety of assessment methods, including traditional paper and pencil tests, as well as projects (like those in a science fair or perhaps a mixed media presentation), new products (such as an original screenplay, a literary magazine, or a sample brochure) or portfolios (a collection of work) to show student achievement. Things can go haywire when educators use only one assessment method — whether traditional or innovative.

Look also for assessment methods that appear (in commonsense terms) to fit the target. You should worry when a physical education teacher uses a multiple-choice test to measure physical fitness, when a performing arts teacher bases an entire grade on a true/false test of art history, or when a foreign language teacher fails to rely, at least in part, on performance assessments to see if students can communicate effectively. In short, even those of us untrained in the complexities of classroom assessment should see common sense at work in our children's classrooms.

Appropriate sampling

The classroom teacher's dilemma in this case challenges them to gather enough information to be able to draw confident conclusions about each student's achievement without going overboard. The most important things to analyze here are the number and types of assessment opportunities. To be able to judge a person's proficiency at anything (a golf swing, ability to tell a story, artistic talent) often we need to see them do it more than once. How many times do you want a commercial pilot to land an airplane successfully before being certified to fly? More than one or two to be sure — and we'd like those demonstrations to sample the ability to land under varied weather conditions.

The school version of this example is, How many different times must a teacher see a student write proficiently to confidently conclude that that student is a good writer? More than one or two to be sure — and the teacher would like the student to demonstrate skill with a number of different kinds of writing.

Errors can occur when any single episode serves as the basis for evaluating someone's capabilities. Sound practice involves repeated assessments, sometimes all at one time (a multiple-choice test including many items) and other times spread over time (a term-length writing journal).

"Sound practice involves repeated assessments!"

We know of a high school biology teacher who confronted a sampling challenge. This teacher relied on the unit exams published with a newly adopted biology text. She noticed that many students (including her highest achievers) were struggling on these tests, even though they seemed to do well on daily work and in class discussions. Finally, in desperation, the teacher carefully analyzed what the tests tested. To her horror, she found that both the text and her instruction were preparing students to reason and solve problems in biology, while the tests emphasized memorization and regurgitation of disconnected facts.

The tests sampled different targets than those the students and teacher were emphasizing. The teacher acted immediately to supplement the tests with her own reasoning exercises.

As another example, here is an all too common sampling problem, particularly in elementary schools: many music, art, and physical education teachers are given teaching assignments spanning several schools in a given week. They pop in, replace several regular teachers for an hour in each classroom, carry out planned activities, and move quickly on to the next school. As a result, they may face several hundred different students in a given week — none for more than an hour or so. Clearly, they are not given enough time to learn who all their students are, let alone to sample their performance. Yet, at the end of the semester, they are expected to assign a report card grade to each of these several hundred students. Their assessment, evaluation and grading challenge is insurmountable. For each child, there appears on the report card an utterly and completely undependable grade. *Grading policies that give rise to unsound assessment must be changed.*

Sampling problems can accompany the use of standardized tests, too. Remember that we have described four kinds of achievement targets: mastery of content knowledge, learning to use that knowledge to solve problems, developing performance skills, and learning to use those skills to create products that meet standards of quality. The commercially published standardized achievement tests typically used in local district testing programs and reported annually to the school board and in newspapers rely on multiple-choice test items that sample just two of these four targets: knowledge and reasoning. Performance skills and product development capabilities are ignored. The problem is that many parents and communities believe that they can evaluate the quality of schools on the basis of these test scores alone — scores on tests that *fail to reflect* two of the four kinds of achievement required of students.

Parents concerned about the quality of schools are justified in asking to hear the rest of the story. Assessing skill and product targets such as the ability to write well requires performance assessments. So we might expect these kinds of assessments to accompany annual multiple-choice standardized tests.

Moms and dads who have become critical consumers of information about achievement ask questions about the nature and scope of the targets sampled in determining report card grades or test scores. Red flags should go up if the teacher has no sampling plan to share or when the sampling plan doesn't seem to make common sense.

Avoiding bias

Critical consumers of achievement information also understand that clear targets, proper assessment methods, and appropriate samples of student work do not guarantee accurate assessment. Even with all of these keys to success in place, other things can cause assessment problems.

For example, problems can arise from within the student, such as ill health, emotional upset, or a lack of language proficiency that can bias assessment results and lead to incorrect conclusions about achievement. Problems can arise from within the test itself, such as culturally biased test items, poorly written items, or inadequate instructions. And, problems can arise from the environment within which the test is administered, including everything from noise and other distractions during testing to unqualified evaluators reading and judging student work.

To understand the nature of biased test items, consider the plight of students raised in home cultures in which children are taught to show respect for elders by remaining silent. If these children are then placed in classrooms in which grades are based at least in part on active participation in class discussion, they are placed at a systematic disadvantage. Teachers who infer a lack of achievement from these students' lack of involvement may be making an error. This represents biased assessment.

Or, consider the case of a standardized test item that requires knowing the number of legs on a chicken. Students from a rural environment have little difficulty here. But what about the urban second grader whose only experience with chickens has involved those supermarket packages, where chickens are routinely packed with four legs?

To be sure, careful teachers can avoid almost all of these sources of potential bias. Table 3.1 lists examples of potential bias and possible countermeasures. Your child's teacher should know these things and understand how to avoid them.

Please note that your job is *not* to try to detect bias in your child's assessments. That is a technical matter requiring professional expertise. Your task is not to fix the problem. Rather, once again in this case, your challenge is to see if teachers are aware of issues of assessment bias and of countermeasures. Your assignment is to wonder aloud to those in positions of authority what might be done by way of professional development to help teachers avoid potential problems. Again, diplomacy is paramount.

Table 3.1
Promoting Accurate Assessment by Minimizing Potential Problems

POTENTIAL PROBLEMS	REASON FOR CONCERN	COUNTERMEASURES
Giving a multiple-choice test to a nonreader	May know material and still score low	Develop their reading skills or read the test to students
Giving as essay test to a nonwriter	May know material and still score low	Develop writing skills or use other method
Poor health or emotional upset at test time	May be unable to concentrate	Retest at another time
Noise or other distractions during testing	May be unable to concentrate	Plan ahead for a quiet environment or retest
Poorly worded test questions	May misunderstand questions	Learn in advance to write clear questions
Clues in items that give answers away	May answer correctly for wrong reason	Recognize and eliminate clues in advance
Incorrect test scoring key	Items answered right but marked wrong	Double check for accuracy
Lack of clear standards for judging	Inconsistent ratings of performance	Plan scoring standards in advance
Cultural bias in test items	Some students placed at disadvantage	Find and eliminate bias in advance
Ethnic or gender bias in the evaluator	Some students placed at disadvantage	Recognize and eliminate stereotypes in advance

Are we communicating effectively about student success?

The following conditions are critical for us to communicate effectively about student achievement:

- Teachers must use quality assessments to determine achievement.

- Results must be transformed into terms (grades or scores) whose meaning both message sender (most often the teacher) and receiver (student, parent, etc.) understand.

- The message sender must check to ensure this proper understanding.

In other words, the message gets through when both parties consistently and accurately understand the meaning of the symbols used.

Teachers typically rely on a variety of ways to communicate, including grades, test scores, portfolios, narrative reports, and parent or student conferences of various types. All must meet the stated conditions to be effective. When teachers use quality assessments to generate rich detail about student achievement, most soon realize how helpful a complete portrait of the achievements of their students can be. They also realize that no single reporting strategy can meet everyone's needs. This is because different ways of reporting achievement information present different amounts of detail.

For example, a onetime snapshot (or a single grade) cannot tell parents about growth over time, relative strengths and weaknesses, or performance relative to the teacher's important

"No single reporting strategy can meet everyone's needs."

achievement standards. For these reasons, some districts are developing new reporting formats that include more information about student attainment of expected skills. These include more detailed report cards, portfolios, and new conference techniques.

A *portfolio* is a collection of student work assembled for the purpose of describing either that student's achievement status at a point in time or growth in achievement over time. To make this reporting strategy work, teachers must start with a clear set of achievement expectations and share that vision with their students, along with a vocabulary that will permit students to communicate about their successes. Further, teachers must use the classroom assessment process to keep students in touch with improvements in their performance and provide them with a vocabulary that will permit them to communicate about that. In short, the process of preparing students to reflect intelligently about their own achievement may represent one of the most powerfully focused forms of instruction available to teachers. Most report that students are highly motivated to tell stories of their own successes.

Another exciting option actually allows students to lead parents through a conference in partnership with their teacher. These types of "student-led" conferences require students to examine and analyze their own growth over time in relation to the teacher's standards in order to explain what they have learned. By taking a lead role in this process, students can become much more connected to and therefore more responsible for their own performance (or lack thereof). The pride in accomplishment students feel when they have a positive message to deliver at a conference, and when they deliver it well, is something to behold!

"Students can become much more . . . responsible for their own performance."

Although relatively new, this practice is catching on across the United States and Canada. We'll tell you at the end of the guide where you can learn more about it. Of course, these kinds of conferences are not foolproof. They can be done well or badly. Teachers must master specific craft knowledge to use them well. Thus, once again, professional development is key to teachers' success.

By and large, you can have confidence in the communication practices used in your child's school when the following are true:

- You receive reports about the achievement of your child regularly enough to satisfy your needs.

- The information you receive is at least somewhat consistent with your own understanding of your child's level of achievement or progress.

- The district or school checks with you regularly to see what kinds of information about student achievement you would like to receive.

- Teachers and administrators meet to plan specific strategies to meet those needs.

- Teachers communicate regularly and effectively with their students about progress in relation to expectations.

- Grades on report cards or standardized test scores are accompanied by interpretive aids to help you understand what they mean.

You should be concerned if any of these occur haphazardly or not at all.

Report card grades as communication

Report cards and grades hold a special place both in our school culture and in our larger society. In addition to their role in communication, in the minds of many, they represent the rewards and punishments that motivate students. Because of the importance they command, they deserve special attention in your critical evaluation of school practices.

First, you must never lose sight of the fact the *grades teachers assign are only as sound as the assessments used to gather the achievement information.* If the underlying achievement targets are unclear or the assessments are of poor quality (due to reliance on inappropriate methods, unsound sampling, or test bias), then the resulting grades will not accurately reflect your child's level of attainment. Interpretable grades must be based on accurate assessments.

Second, we all remember from our youth that a number of different factors seemed to find their way into the determination of a final grade. Certainly, achievement was always the key. But in addition, depending on the particular teacher, our level of achievement in relation to our "ability," our level of effort, our overall classroom attitude, and compliance with classroom rules could "count" toward our final grades, too. Our collective school experience notwithstanding, there is reason for you to be very cautious here. Such grade pollution can have very undesirable consequences.

To the extent that different teachers permit different factors to count in grading, define them differently, and assess and weight them in different ways, our simple five-symbol (A through F)

> *"Grades . . . are only as sound as the assessments used to gather the . . . information."*

grade-based communication system can hold within it a great deal of hidden and unrecoverable information. Subtle differences in the actual underlying meaning built into the grade by the "message sender" (teacher) simply cannot be sorted out by those who seek to understand that message (students and parents). Teachers restricted to five letter grades cannot convey the depth of information and nuance of meaning their ongoing academic records contain for each student. When the objective is effective communication, the remedy is to encourage schools to adopt grading policies that permit teachers to indicate each student's current level of academic achievement with nothing else factored in to interfere with that message. Teachers would then accompany that with separate information about other relevant student characteristics (effort, attitude, compliance, behavior, etc.).

Further, consistent with the basic message of this entire guide, parents should seek assurance that teachers adhere to the same standards of assessment quality specified here for achievement when they assess effort, attitude, or behavior. If we cannot be assured of the quality of assessment of these nonachievement factors, then teachers and schools have no business reporting them in any form.

As parents, the one student characteristic we should request is a completely clear and untainted indication of the student's current level of achievement in each subject that student is studying. If schools have quality information about those other factors and wish to report them, that's fine. But they should report them separately on the report card.

The bottom line is that there are basic principles of sound report card grading. Adhere to these principles and effective communication is possible. Violate them and we ensure miscommunication about student achievement. Standards of effective grading practice need to be reflected in district grading policies and in the actual implementation of those policies in classrooms. As parents, we can ask key questions to see if they are.

Standardized test scores as communication

Almost every school district conducts an annual standardized testing program. Almost every state now conducts an annual statewide testing program. In addition, many schools participate in national and even international testing programs. To see how they fit into the big picture of school assessment, we must understand their purposes, the kinds of achievements they assess, the manner in which they assess, and the meaning of the resulting test scores.

Remember, these once-a-year tests are designed to meet the information needs of those who make policy-level decisions about the effectiveness of schools. At the state level, that means the state department of education and those legislators who allocate resources for schools. At the district level, it means the school board, superintendent, curriculum director, and so on. Because these tests happen so infrequently, teachers faced with the need to make decisions continually are not likely to find them helpful. These tests are designed for use at levels outside the classroom.

Tests used in typical districtwide testing programs tend to reflect very broad achievement targets, often covering several years worth of academic material in a single test. For instance, one test might cover three grade levels of math material in one set of 45 test items. Thus, the test developer has just 15 items available to cover a year's worth of material. The result will be very broad, very shallow coverage.

Further, remember that many published standardized tests — the kind typically purchased for districtwide testing programs — evaluate content and reasoning proficiencies only. Performance skills and products are not tested. We point this out again to be sure parents understand that we cannot judge the quality of schools on the basis of these test scores alone. They may reflect only half (albeit an important half) of the achievement targets valued in schools. Keep standardized test scores in perspective. Commercial standardized tests rely on just one of our four available assessment formats: multiple-choice items. To get a complete portrait of the big achievement picture, evidence of student performance on the remaining targets must come from other classroom or district testing methods.

We urge you to keep these tests in perspective. They are highly visible and appear to carry great weight in the schooling process. Considerable pressure for both teachers and students is typically associated with their use. Just remember that, even with their obvious political and media appeal, they represent only a fraction of one percent of the assessments students experience in school. The rest happen in the classroom under the control of their teachers. Further, while standardized tests certainly do inform important decision makers, it is those *day-to-day classroom assessments* that inform students, teachers, and parents. We keep standardized tests in perspective when we understand that they make small contributions to a very large assessment picture in schools.

"Standardized tests ... make small contributions to a very large assessment picture."

You must be careful when interpreting the scores that come from district testing programs. They are easy to misunderstand. For example, one score popular with parents is the *grade equivalent score*. This score conveys student performance in years and months, such as 3.5 in math, meaning third grade, fifth month. The danger here is that some parents think that this test tests a set of proficiencies in mathematics that are always covered in third grade. If their third grader scores at this level, that child is mastering those proficiencies. This is wrong. All the score means is that this child answered the same number of items right on this test as did other students who took the test in the middle of third grade. Thus, the score compares students to one another, and that's all. It does *not* compare students to a preestablished set of standards.

Percentile scores can be another source of confusion. For example, your child may receive a percentile score of 75. This does not mean the student answered 75 percent of the items correctly; that would be *percent correct*. The *percentile score* means that your child outscored 75 percent of the students who took the test at about this time in their education. Again, it compares your child to other students.

Finally, be advised that many state assessments provide for a different kind of interpretation of results. Often they are developed to reflect student attainment of specific academic proficiencies, and thus *do* compare student scores to preestablished standards. For example, such tests ask if the examinee has answered enough questions right to lead to the conclusion that that student has mastered a set of specific reading or writing proficiencies. How they compare to other students is not relevant in this context. Typically, these tests provide greater detail about student achievement, going beyond content and reasoning to include skill and product targets relying on a broader array of assessment methods. Nevertheless, their scores require careful interpretation, too.

To ensure effective communication using any standardized test scores, ask your child's teachers to provide you with an explanation you understand and can paraphrase back to them. If you are at all unsure of the explanation, ask the principal or the district's assessment specialist to help you understand. But above all, do not relent in your inquiry unless and until you know and completely understand what was tested and how your child performed.

A comment on intelligence testing

Adults of our generation grew up in a culture that believed that we were born with an *intelligence quotient*, or IQ. This indicator of intellectual ability was genetically determined, cast in stone, and limited our achievement potential in all contexts. While we still acknowledge differences in intellectual capabilities, and while cognitive psychologists still believe that students vary in potential academic attainment in school, be careful when assessing and dealing with IQ in schools today.

The reasons are many. First, there is fundamental disagreement among leading scholars around the world today as to whether we each have one or several IQs. There is evidence that intelligence takes many different forms within each of us, yielding a profile of strengths and weaknesses.

"Intelligence takes many different forms within each of us, yielding a profile of strengths and weaknesses."

Further, there is fundamental disagreement regarding whether IQ is a stable or changeable human characteristic. Noted scholars point to instructional interventions that appear to have a profound impact on intelligence. Some contend that IQ is changeable during the early formative years but becomes more stable with age.

In addition, the relationship between intelligence and achievement is not clear. Some researchers have demonstrated very high levels of achievement in very technical disciplines (math and science) among students whose IQ scores suggest such attainments would not be possible.

For all of these reasons, we urge extreme caution in the administration and use of intelligence tests. Certainly extremely high or low scores on such tests deserve special attention. Such students may indeed have special needs requiring individualized instructional programs. But in the middle range there is a danger that IQ scores can become excuses for not holding students to high standards, not searching out and building on their strengths, or not striving to motivate students to aspire to academic success. The result can be students who fail to reach their fullest potential or students who lose confidence in themselves as learners.

Until cognitive psychologists sort out fact from fiction and mythology about intelligence as a human characteristic and its relationship to achievement, it is prudent to assess and make decisions on the basis of the student's *demonstrated* level of achievement versus an undependable indicator of "potential."

"IQ scores can become excuses for not holding students to high standards."

Summary: Remaining alert to issues of quality

Quality assessment, evaluation, and communication are essential for our children's academic well-being. Clear standards of quality practice exist, which we examined in Chapter 2. However, many practicing educators have not been given access to these standards. There is reason for parents to wonder aloud if local schools and districts should allocate resources for professional development in the service of sound assessment practices.

The purpose of this chapter has been to outline some of the danger signals. As you visit schools and classrooms and as you ask questions about assessment, evaluation, and grading practices, you should find yourself wondering the following:

- What achievement targets drive instruction?

- Are those targets integrated across classrooms and grade levels?

- Whose information needs are the assessment results meeting?

- Do the assessment methods being used really fit the teacher's achievement expectations?

- Do sampling procedures promise dependable information?

- Are assessments of student achievement likely to be relatively bias free?

It's good to wonder. It's good to ask. And it's good to support action in your schools on behalf of meeting standards of sound assessment practice. In the fourth and final chapter, we suggest concrete ways you can to just that.

What can parents do to help?

As members of the school community, parents, teachers, and administrators usually have the same big goals — good schools where sound programs lead to proven learning. Despite this common desire, it's also true that complex problems often seem overwhelming to any one of these groups.

For example, a school system can often seem very large, threatening or insular to parents. There are so many people to contact; so many layers of authority, and many times the educators seem to be completely immersed in their own culture. Likewise, teachers and administrators often feel that they are being asked to take on more problems, respond to more reform agendas, and generate more plans for change. All of this is supposed to happen with few additional resources and certainly no extra time for reflection or planning.

Given these frustrating conditions, it's not surprising that you may be wondering, "If I'm a parent who wants to help change the face of assessment, what do I do next? How can I get close enough to hope to improve things? How can I be taken seriously? How do I even know where to start? And, if I raise the issue of quality assessment with my child's teachers, do I risk damaging my child's relationship to them?"

This final chapter is designed to help answer some of these questions. Even though schools and school-related issues are complex and often intimidating, you can take action to make a positive difference by supporting movement toward excellence in assessment. While the task of improving overall assessment practices is large and challenging, it can also be broken into smaller, more "doable" pieces.

Power in partnerships

Before looking at these possibilities, let's discuss for a moment the tone you may choose to adopt. Throughout the course of any of your actions, you will likely be communicating with a variety of school personnel. It is important to remember that these people are often on the receiving end of a barrage of needs, concerns, and even complaints. In this context, it may be true that the squeaky (or even persistent) wheel gets the grease. However, when you decide to address a need (to "squeak," if you will), then it's wise to remember that if your tone is positive, respectful, and proactive, you will greatly increase your chances for success.

"Long-term, significant change requires a sincere, team effort."

By all means, voice your ideas in clear and firm ways. But remember that, in essence, your task will be to *persuade* individuals to reexamine perhaps basic assumptions, and if necessary change their behavior as a result. This is no easy task. Long-term, significant change requires a sincere, team effort. Changing assessment practices will require the help of classroom teachers, principals, district office support staff, and likely board members.

Most school improvement research indicates that changes motivated by fear, pressure, or intimidation are likely to be short term and fairly cosmetic. This is not good enough. If you are willing and interested in forming an assessment partnership with your local school, then it is worth your time and effort to develop good approach strategies. These include finding ways to get and keep the attention of key players, knowing who to contact for which purposes, and using ideas to maintain the momentum of your work. Later in this chapter you will receive specific tips and starter ideas to use at a variety of levels in schools. Before getting to these techniques, however, it's important for you to understand the actual needs of your school district.

Focus your involvement

Remember that you are looking for evidence that your schools are part of a high-quality performing system. If quality instruction and assessment practices are obviously linked to high student performance, then you'll just want to sustain what's already working. Most likely you can be the greatest help if you publicly recognize good work and then stay out of the way.

If, however, you survey the landscape and see obvious gaps, then your effort will require some type of strategic involvement, which may or may not require lots of careful planning and time. It's important to tailor your actions to valid needs. How can you zero in on these?

First, you can consider using the following Needs Assessment Checklists. These checklists consist of simple questions targeted at two important areas. The first is your child's classroom — obviously the place where it's easiest to collect information.

In fact, if you see nothing but positive evidence at this level, you may want to stop here. The second checklist looks for information most often found at the district level. Again, answering these questions should be fairly easy if you contact your district administration office for assistance. By working through these checklists you should quickly collect data and examples to guide your next steps.

Looking into your child's classroom

Use the following checklists to see what you can learn about the assessment climate in your child's classroom. In the next section, we suggest ways for you to approach your child's teacher.

Table 4.1 Needs Checklist at the Classroom Level

REASONABLE QUESTIONS TO ASK ABOUT THE PRACTICES IN YOUR CHILD'S CLASSROOM	EVIDENCE OR EXAMPLES YOU ARE LIKELY TO SEE IF THINGS ARE GOING WELL
Can the teacher articulate targets and expectations for learning?	*A concise lists of content, reasoning, skills, products, or projects for each student to master (in each subject taught)* ■ *Easy-to-read curriculum summaries* ■ *Report procedures keyed directly back to these curriculum goals.*
Can the teacher provide examples of high-quality work?	*Samples of student work showing exemplary performance on typical classroom assignments, projects, or exams* ■ *Reports from your child that teacher uses lots of examples to "show" what's expected.*

Table 4.1 Needs Checklist at the Classroom Level, continued

REASONABLE QUESTIONS...	EVIDENCE OR EXAMPLES...
Are you and your child aware of standards of quality for student work?	*Expectations and overall evaluation plans clearly communicated to kids and parents ▪ For parents, information about this is sent home or is reviewed at parent conferences or on parent nights ▪ For students, teacher routinely covers expectations and standards at the beginning of an assignment or unit.*
Does the teacher seem to be familiar with basic assessment vocabulary and practices as outlined in this guide?	*When asked about "assessment practices" the teacher has clearly thought about his or her ideas ▪ Teacher seems to be familiar with various types of assessment (e.g., classroom and standardized; right answer, essay, and performance-based) ▪ Teacher has a clear philosophy related to assessment ▪ Teacher can explain how he or she uses assessment in connection with various kinds of achievement.*
Is a mix of assessment strategies used in the class?	*You hear about or see examples of a range of assessment practices ▪ Could include traditional multiple-choice tests as well as projects, presentations, exhibitions, performances, essays, etc.*
Is your child involved in assessing his or her own achievement?	*Your child gets to see and understand scoring criteria ▪ Is asked to evaluate her or his own performance on some tasks ▪ Is encouraged to keep track of performance and overall progress ▪ Sometimes students might be involved in parent-teacher conferences.*
Is your child clear about his or her own achievement?	*Student can explain how grades are determined ▪ Can identify descriptors and examples of excellent, fair, poor work ▪ Knows where he or she stands relative to what teacher expects.*

Table 4.1 Needs Checklist at the Classroom Level, continued

REASONABLE QUESTIONS . . .	EVIDENCE OR EXAMPLES . . .
Does the teacher rely on a variety of ways to communicate about achievement?	*Possibilities include report cards, checklists, rating scales, portfolios, student-parent-teacher, student-teacher, and student-led conferences ▪ Methods of communication make sense given information to be shared.*
Is your child's teacher aware of various sources of bias in assessment?	*Teacher should know how to prevent bias in tests and in observations of students.*

Table 4.2 Needs Checklist at the District Level

REASONABLE QUESTIONS TO ASK ABOUT THE PRACTICES AT THE DISTRICT LEVEL	EVIDENCE OR EXAMPLES YOU ARE LIKELY TO SEE IF THINGS ARE GOING WELL
Does the district have a definitive, written curriculum with clear learning targets coordinated across grade levels for parents to review?	*Published curriculum guides ▪ Concise learning objectives identified for various levels of development.*
Is there a comprehensive staff training plan related to assessment and other types of instructional improvement?	*A list of staff training options at the building or district level ▪ Principals can talk about specific training experiences they have promoted for their teachers.*
Does district have written assessment philosophy acknowledging the need for quality and outlining how assessment fits into the classroom learning process?	*School board should have endorsed such a policy ▪ Copies should be available.*
Is there a comprehensive plan for standardized testing within the district, or a statement of rationale?	*These tests serve purposes when kept in perspective and when used by policy makers, administrators, and planners who know their strengths and limits. They should be part of a bigger plan.*

Diplomacy: How to approach your "partner"

Let's assume that you've reviewed the checklist and would like to pursue some of these questions, particularly with the classroom teacher. Naturally your first thoughts will be about how to approach this person. Remember, your goal is to build a partnership where everyone can honestly examine ideas and issues with a team focus on the child. It's helpful to think in advance about how to make that initial contact. You might even want to role play this in your mind or work with an idea outline. To help you along, look at the following Do's and Don'ts lists. Of course you'll want to use your own words, but these prompts may give you some good ideas.

"Your goal is to build a partnership ... with a team focus on the child."

Ways to phrase your initial inquiries (Do's)

"I've been trying to update my own knowledge and reading related to schools. I've got some questions about the whole area of assessment. Could you help me understand how you work with this in your classroom?"

— *or* "As an interested parent, I enjoy working closely with teachers on a number of topics that affect my child. One of these topics is assessment — getting a handle on what kids learn. Would it be all right if we found a time to sit down and discuss your ideas on assessment?"

— *or* "Recently I received this book for parents written about assessment in schools. It's raised a number of questions for me. I'd like to talk to an educator about them. Would you be willing to meet with me sometime and discuss my questions?"

Approaches sure to backfire (Don'ts)

"I'm very concerned about some of the shortfalls I see in education, especially about assessment. I have some very specific questions about this area, and I would like some answers from you about your own practices. When can we meet?"

— *or* "Recently I received a list of things I should watch for in my child's classroom. Several of these things relate to testing and assessment. I will be asking you to show me examples from your teaching to see how you match up to this list."

— *or* "Here's a list of things I will want to watch for this year as I observe in Billy's classroom. I'd like for you to collect some samples from your past years of teaching and be prepared to explain to me how you address these areas."

As tactless as some of these second examples may seem, they are all real-life comments made to teachers. Most parents naturally will use common sense when they talk with school personnel. Nevertheless, it's quite helpful to shape your queries ahead of time. Using the right tone can open the door to fruitful, ongoing dialogue.

Levels of involvement

If you've conducted your own personal needs assessment and determined that assessment quality could be a focus of improvement at your local school, then you also need to plan how to successfully make your case. This is essentially a teaching task. As we discussed in Chapter 1, all good teaching plans are like road maps — they contain beginning points, routes of progress, and destinations. Your goal is to educate people and persuade them to share your view. To get started, think about the level of involvement you might want to commit to. As you discerned from the previous section, the logical place to start is with children and teachers. For one thing, you have more access to your child than anyone else in this process. For another, it is only the interaction of children and teachers that really matters in learning. So, let's open the map, begin at the beginning, and talk about involvement strategies that have some real chance of working.

1. Working with your child

Although your child is probably your most valuable source of information, it's also true that many parents often skip to other levels of involvement before tapping their own precious resources. Students are the essential key in analyzing the assessment climate of any classroom. This is because it is their experiences and behaviors that will most reliably reflect the true workings of day-to-day instruction. So be ready to employ two key strategies as you interact with your kids: Make it a practice to *listen* and to *probe*.

The old adage that children never talk about what they've learned in school can seem true until you begin to listen closely to the nuances of their conversations. When students talk to you about school (and especially when they talk to each other), it's likely that the fragmented topics or bits of information about issues or problems or classroom goings on will begin to paint a picture of daily classroom routine. More than likely those themes that appear often, or are repeated, represent key events, important areas of emphasis or values that your child has internalized.

"Make it a practice to listen and to probe."

For example, a kindergartner may point out a pattern in a poster border and comment that they have been studying patterns in math. Or your fourth grader, while talking to a friend, may excitedly describe the various characters her classmates chose to represent when they did their oral book reports. These casual remarks about work that they bring home are usually windows into the assessment workings of the classroom as children interpret them. Children tend to comment on things they have somehow catalogued as important, interesting, or necessary to remember. By listening for these recurring snippets and especially by asking follow-up questions (probing), you can begin to get a fairly accurate picture of classroom priorities, practices, and routines.

It's also important to note that not everything children say is important or necessarily accurate. Parents know that children are exuberant, colorful, and excitable creatures who occasionally like to exaggerate. That's why follow-up questions and interested probes (for the whole picture) are so critical.

And remember, you can ask your child direct questions about matters of importance, such as, "Does your teacher expect you to know this or to be able to look it up?" "If your teacher is going to observe and evaluate your skill performance, did she make the basis of the observation [the standards] clear?" "How many times has the teacher had you do this and how often [sampling question]?" [For nonreaders] "Did someone read the test to you?"

Similarly, you can even provide your child with direct questions to ask her or his teacher to protect the child's interests: "Can you remind me about what I'm supposed to know?" "Can you tell me once again about how I solve problems like this?"

"What performance skills am I going to need to master, if any, to succeed?" "Exactly what factors will go into determining my grade?" "What is the assessment plan for determining my grade?"

But as you and your child converse, you should expect to hear comments about grading practices, different types of assignments, reactions to assessment and management practices and, most importantly, comments about the child's sense of success and empowerment in the classroom. Think of these kernels of information as the initial artifacts in an archeological dig or the beginning pieces of evidence in an important detective investigation. By moving on to the next step you can decide which pieces of information are the really valuable things that you may want to discuss with the teacher.

"What factors will go into determining my grade?"

2. Working with your child's teacher

Whether it's based on work with their children or just on normal parental curiosity and involvement, almost every parent will eventually interact with their children's teachers. If your involvement is going to focus on assessment and curriculum, the following pointers can increase your chances for success.

We have already discussed how to make that initial approach with an instructor. Remember, the focus here is on building partnerships. The following ideas can help you sustain a positive focus on assessment quality throughout the year.

Parent conferences. Make the best use of regularly scheduled parent conferences. This is the forum where teachers naturally expect you to ask questions about class protocol and curriculum, and is a logical place to address issues found in this chapter's Needs Assessment Checklists. In scheduled conferences, you should expect to see samples of student work and performance data about your child. In this context, it's natural to direct the conversation towards assessment practices. You can ask the teacher to explain grading practices, to show you the learning goals for a semester, or to explain the way he or she plans to evaluate your child's progress. Most importantly, be sure you've thought through these types of questions ahead of time. Decide which topics you want to address and think about how to communicate your interest in assessment with that particular teacher. You might broach the topic of future student involvement in conferences.

Personal notes. Another powerful tool you can use is the personal note. Like all of us, teachers need to hear about the things they're doing right. For example, if you are particularly impressed with the criteria for a certain assignment or if you realize that your child is very clear about the learning targets for a current unit, then let the teacher hear about it. By highlighting specific examples and applauding them in a short, personalized note you can dramatically reinforce positive practices. Chances are high that teachers will feel good about repeating these behaviors. A simple note (or even a telephone call) can make a teacher's whole day! And, of course, you can use such notes to ask simple questions about assessment and grading practices, too.

Develop a "sharing pipeline." Like the quick note, an effort to share one or two ideas at a time can also be an effective strategy. Here's how this might work: Suppose you read a good article about using portfolios in a language arts class, or a friend tells you about a well-organized social studies project her child experienced at another school. Teachers are always looking for good ideas. Make it a practice to share this type of information (in condensed, easy-to-read or understandable format) informally with your child's instructor. Tell her or him that you thought they might be interested — which is why you're passing the information along. Sometimes you might also want to send a copy to the principal if you have something in writing. If these efforts are made in a casual, upbeat fashion, you can quickly establish a positive pipeline of communication between home and school.

Volunteering: The ultimate connection. Finally, volunteering can be one of the most effective ways to positively affect the assessment climate in your child's classroom. Even if you end up running copies of materials or working on bulletin boards, it's amazing the insights you can glean from just a few hours "in the building." You will be surprised how much more you'll know about the day-to-day details of instruction after only a small amount of time in your child's classroom or even in other parts of the school. Soon, you'll get a feel for the teacher's classroom management style, daily rules, typical daily lessons, priorities of a particular grade level, and assessment practices. With this enriched contextual background, you'll find it much easier to make informed observations.

In addition, closer proximity to both teacher and classroom will make it easier to chat with key people in the building. Like many parents, you may find that your job or schedule makes on-site volunteering difficult or impossible. Don't discard the concept altogether, however. Maybe you can help with some projects at home. Just the simple act of offering your services can be the beginning of greater communication.

3. Involving the principal

If you decide that quality assessment should be a priority in your schools, then at some time you may want to explore the topic with the principal. Even if you are communicating with individual teachers on a regular basis, you will also want to touch base with the building administrator. This is important because the principal is charged with instructional leadership in a building, and is the conduit for most important decisions and policies affecting all teachers and grade levels. If practices at a site are going to become pervasive, then almost always the principal is involved.

Always remember, your purpose in this case is to be sure teachers receive the resources and support they need in the classroom to do a sound job of assessing and communicating. If time for professional development or added materials are needed to do a good job, the principal is the person who must secure them. This partnership is essential, too.

The easiest way to cultivate principal involvement is simply to include him or her in your normal communication loop. You can use the same methods (personal notes, talking up good ideas, volunteering) to share information with a teacher and the principal at the same time. For example, if you send a positive note to a teacher about one of his grading practices, send a courtesy copy to the principal. Not only will the administrator appreciate this feedback, but the teacher will be thrilled to know that you shared good news with his supervisor! Similarly, if you are volunteering in a school, you will find it easy to stop and chat with the principal in the hall or as you pass by the office.

Even in very good schools, however, there may also be times when you need to share potential problems with the principal. Suppose your analysis of the assessment climate in a particular classroom has led you to be concerned — maybe the grading criteria are fuzzy or perhaps the teacher is relying on only one limited type of assessment. Sometimes your concerns may be heightened if you have tried to talk with the teacher but were unsuccessful. Whatever the case, at some point you may wonder when and how to involve the principal. Here are some suggestions.

First, remember that in a professional setting, it's a common courtesy to begin at the beginning. *If you are concerned about a certain teacher's practices or materials, then a direct discussion with that teacher must be the first step.* Teachers understand that parents must be advocates for their children, but they will always prefer dealing directly with the parent rather than with a third party or supervisor.

If this sincere attempt to interact with the teacher is not fruitful, it's probably time to go to the next level. You have several choices. You might want to begin by talking informally with the principal, sharing your concerns but indicating that you do not want to personalize the situation. Sometimes, this will allow the principal to deal with the topic in a general fashion with the entire staff — perhaps through some type of staff training or faculty meeting discussion. If you feel that circumstances are such that more immediate action is called for, then you should indicate this. Remember, however, that a serious complaint from a parent usually gets back to the teacher. Administrators cannot usually discuss concerns in a vacuum, so you should be

"Direct discussion with that teacher must be the first step."

prepared for eventual principal–teacher feedback. You may wish to open by suggesting a joint conference involving you, the teacher, and the principal. This way everyone is hearing the same information at the same time and resulting solutions can be put into effect more quickly. Again, many teachers prefer this more direct approach even if it seems initially uncomfortable.

Whether your contact with the principal is one on one or also involves a teacher, it's also a good idea to build in a follow-up step. Indicate that you'd like to revisit the issue at some predetermined time in the future. Explain that all of you can review progress and make any necessary adjustments. This scheduled follow-up meeting builds in more accountability for everyone, and helps ensure that busy schedules won't destroy good intentions.

In all of these situations, remember that a good principal should work to provide service to both parents and teachers. Principals can be a terrific resource, and you should feel comfortable calling on their help.

4. Involvement at the district level

Even as they work with building teachers and principals, the most effective parent change agents soon learn how to affect policy and practice at the district level. A little digging should easily reveal how you can experience this kind of involvement.

First, try to find out which districtwide committees meet regularly and include parent representatives. Most districts have curriculum-oriented committees that work to select new textbooks and make recommendations about program changes. These forums are a natural for input related to assessment. Also look for parent advisory committees that meet with the superintendent or serve as a liaison group to the school board. The best way to find out about these groups is to contact the district or administration office directly. Call the superintendent's office and inquire about parent involvement on committees and the application process for such groups. Most school districts are actively looking for participants, so a little perseverance and interest should quickly pay off.

If you're willing to donate your time and energy to these efforts, it's also a good idea to try to find some kindred spirits who are willing to do the same. Look for other parents who share your commitment to improving the instruction and assessment environment. Not only is it more comfortable to make suggestions as part of a concerned team, it's probably also more effective.

One other essential ingredient for improving teaching practices is well-designed training. Remember how we established early on that assessment training is rarely part of the teacher and administrator preparation process? Although this training can sometimes be coordinated by a building principal, it is often directed (or at least funded) by the district office. In your conversations with teachers and principals or via your role as a committee representative, you can encourage this type of training. Teachers need time to hear new ideas, look at practices from other schools, and reflect on ways to integrate new examples into their own classrooms.

Be assured that this type of training does not need to be expensive. Indeed, many districts are discovering that one of the most effective training models is the formation of study groups or learning teams. In this setting, a group of teachers, administrators, and parents often read and discuss a book or articles written about quality assessment. Each group member reads the same materials, and the real benefit comes when insights, ideas, and suggestions are shared collectively. By providing the reference materials and perhaps a weekly facilitator, a district can inexpensively affect a significant number of key people.

5. Involvement at the board level

Your local school board is made up of citizens who have the ultimate responsibility for shaping a district's fiscal and program policies. If you are active on district committees, it's quite likely that your input (via a committee report or recommendation) will reach the board level eventually. Of course, there may be times when you want to more directly influence board decisions. Again consider progressive levels of communication. It can be surprisingly effective to contact board members individually, away from a board meeting setting. Keep them informed about promising practices related to assessment and enlist their support in these efforts. With so many issues now connected with school governance, it's often easier to garner attention if you can make a more personal and enthusiastic contact.

"If parents have concerns, they should work with local administrators first."

Another strategic suggestion involves respecting the natural hierarchy in schools. Remember that principals, central office administrators, and superintendents are hired to administer a complex system. Most of these employees see themselves as public servants whose job is to make things work and to solve problems when necessary. In order to do this, though, they need to be consulted. If parents have strong concerns or wish to promote large-scale change, they should try to work with local administrators first. Often this prompting can set good things in motion. If you have exhausted all these lines of communication and not much has changed, then it may be time to air concerns publicly, with the school board. Even in this scenario, however, any resulting changes will naturally involve many of the same administrators. *If you can establish a feeling of trust and collaboration from the beginning, then your work will be easier and political turmoil can be avoided.*

Final thoughts

In these four brief chapters, we have posed two questions related to the effectiveness of your child's teacher, school, and district: (1) Is your child's achievement being accurately assessed? (2) Are the results of those assessments being effectively communicated and used? Over the decades, we have taken the answers to these questions for granted. Surely, we assume, the answers must be, "Yes!"

However, a careful examination of teacher and administrator training programs and classroom assessment practices suggests at least the possibility that some students may be at risk of inaccurate assessment. This realization may or may not have surprised you. We raise this issue without prejudice and urge that you begin your investigation of the status of assessment in your schools from that same perspective. It may well be that your child's teacher is one of many who do an outstanding job of assessing and using the results. However, it can be risky to your child to assume that this is true. Your child's teacher may need your assistance in getting the resources needed to become a competent, confident assessor. You can help. We have tried to explain how.

We would be remiss in not mentioning the risks inherent in this set of issues from the educator's point of view. Your sensitivity and diplomacy will be key. If you ask about assessment quality and/or encourage your schools to do so, there is a chance that you might uncover a situation that could turn into a public relations problem. These days, many seem bent on attacking schools to advance their own political agendas. This makes educators edgy. By finding potential flaws in classroom assessment or communication, you might provide ammunition for such attacks. That fact makes this a very important but sensitive set of issues.

A corollary result of your inquiry could be embarrassment for your child's teacher. No one likes to admit gaps in professional competence, especially to a valued client like you. Yet this guide suggests that you may put yourself in the position of making someone do just that.

It takes a master of human relations to help others see how they can build on their strengths to overcome their limitations. Assessment expertise is rarely a strength among practicing educators at any level and is almost always a limitation. But this limitation is virtually always accompanied by things teachers and principals do well. As parents, most of us are not equipped to provide needed assessment expertise, nor can we guide educators' pursuit of that expertise. But we can find some strengths in those whom we wish to help. We can stand on a caring platform as we ask questions about quality assessment, and then stay close by to help however we can. The academic well-being of our children and of those students who follow them hangs in the balance.

Parents' resource list

Armstrong, Thomas, *Multiple Intelligences in the Classroom*. Alexandria, VA: Association for Supervision and Curriculum Development, 1994. Presents a practical overview of the concept of intelligence as described in the research of Howard Gardner; translates seven intelligences into classroom applications with perspectives on assessment strategies and options. To order: 703-549-9110, Stock No. 1-94055, $14.95.

Austin, T., *Changing the View: Student-led Parent Conferences*. Portsmouth, NH: Heinemann, 1994. A thoughtfully written handbook on setting up and conducting student-involved communication systems in classrooms. Provides parents with insight on how students can be more involved in assessing their own learning. To order: 800-541-2086, Order # 08818, ISBN 0-435-0881801, $14.50.

Davies, Anne, Caren Cameron, Colleen Politano, & Kathleen Gregory, *Together is Better: Collaborative Assessment, Evaluation & Reporting*. Winnipeg, Canada: Peguis, 1992. Offers a thorough overview of innovative strategies that teachers are using to make their assessments, evaluations, and reporting more manageable for themselves and more effective for students and parents; also clearly describes how to involve students in the self-evaluation process. To order, call Classroom Connections: 800-603-9888, $16.95.

Guskey, Thomas R. (ed.), *Communicating Student Learning. 1996 ASCD Yearbook*. Alexandria, VA: Association for Supervision and Curriculum Development, 1996. A collection of commonsense readings on strategies for delivering information on student achievement to students and parents. To order: 703-549-9110, Stock No. 196000, $21.95.

Hymes, Donald L, Ann E. Chafin, and Peggy Gonder, *The Changing Face of Testing and Assessment: Problems and Solutions*. Arlington, VA: American Association of School Administrators, 1991. An excellent overview of changes occurring in assessment including a look at testing concerns, new alternatives, and school and district issues. Developed for educators but engaging reading for parents also. To order: 703-528-0700, $14.95.

Kohn, Alfie, *Punished by Rewards*. New York: Houghton Mifflin, 1993. A thoughtful and provocative look at the ways we motivate students to engage in academically productive work, with careful attention to how educators use grades and other rewards in place of intrinsic rewards to support learning. To order: 800-225-3362, ISBN 395-65028-3, $16.45.

Stiggins, Richard J., *Student-Centered Classroom Assessment*, 2nd ed. Upper Saddle River, NJ: Merrill/Prentice Hall, 1997. An introduction to sound classroom assessment practice that underscores the importance of assessment in the learning process and gives step-by-step guidance for establishing achievement targets, selecting the most effective assessment methods, and involving students productively in self-assessment. To order, contact Assessment Training Institute: 800-480-3060, $31.50.